Name:

deßeh

Age:

9

Height:

4.1

I was born in:

LeYington Kentucky

My favorite book is:

PHarrpe Potter

The color I wear most is:

Pin drach purple

My favorite brand or designer is:

aeor

WELCOME

You are the future of fashion
and you have something to say!
Are you ready to communicate in a stylish
and cool way? All you'll need is a pencil,
your imagination, and an ordinary day.
As you learn you'll encounter lots of twists
and turns but when you're done your hard
work will "seam" like fun.

Let's go!

Having style goes beyond just looking
good. It is how you piece together your
look with fashion. It's the first thing
people see.

It's easy!

You'll see the following symbols
throughout this book:

DIY: Have a go and Draw It Yourself!

Fashion Facts: Inside knowledge from the front row

Picture Yourself

Sketch or insert a photo of yourself.
Draw outside the lines or color it in!

Get Set to Sketch

Here's what you'll need to start sketching:

- Pencils (regular and color)
- Felt tip color pens
- Charcoal pencil
- Ruler
- Eraser
- Pencil sharpener
- Drawing paper
- Tracing paper

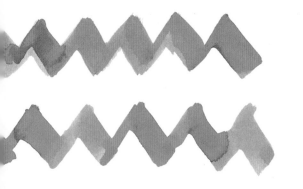

A bit about surface and space...

You can sketch almost anywhere but it's best to sit at a desk or table when you are drawing to do your best. The quality of the surface can affect the outcome of what you sketch.

When you finish, put your sketchbook somewhere safe, like a bookshelf, to protect your work.

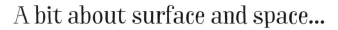

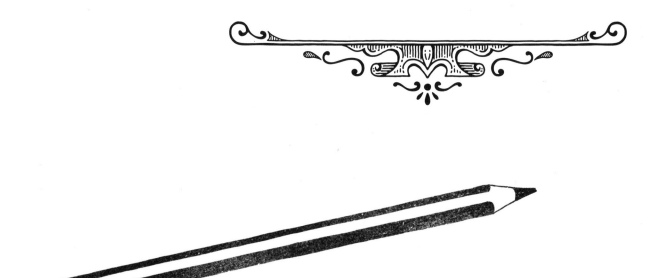

When you're ready,
grab your pencils and
create a color scheme
(and/or pattern) for
this girl's outfit.

Collecting Inspiration

A mood board is a type of collage that is meant to inspire creations like logos, fashion, or even books. Images, text, and other materials are used to create a harmonious composition. Fashion designers use mood boards to help them design their collections from season to season. Making a mood board is typically the first step in their creative process.

Use this list to start gathering interesting materials to create a mood board that will inspire your sketches. Cut and paste the materials you've collected on the next page or in a scrapbook or envelope. Begin building a concept that will later inspire your designs.

- Computer printouts
- Fabric scraps or swatches
- Origami paper
- Tissue paper
- Beads
- Cord
- Feathers
- Pipe cleaners
- Safety pins
- Wrapping paper
- Dried flowers
- Old magazines (for clippings)
- Paint chips (color charts)
- Stickers
- Rhinestones (diamanté)
- Dried leaves
- Lace
- Ribbons
- Wallpaper
- Old birthday cards
- Ornaments
- Grains and beans
- Stamps
- Glitter
- Cereal packets
- Confetti
- Costume jewels
- Yarn or wool
- Washi tape

How to stay organized but surprised:

1. Subscribe to a fashion magazine or visit a newsstand monthly to see what covers catch your eye. It's important to be aware of the trends, even if you don't wear them.

2. Keep a small book of fashion clippings, like swatches, in your tote or purse (handbag).

3. Buy file folders to hold all of your magazine clippings, computer printouts, stickers, and other items that can lay flat.

4. Invest in a simple corkboard and get busy with pinning your inspiration.

5. Turn a boot box into a "cute box"! Decorate a boot box or shoebox and use it to store your file folders and inspiring materials.

Use this page to create your own mood board or collage.

Fill this entire space by drawing something from your mood board. Don't tell your ideas. Show your ideas!

My Favorite Thing

Think of an accessory or clothing item that
you love. It could be your favorite earrings or
a warm cozy sweater.

Describe it. How would it describe you?

_____

_____

_____

_____

_____

_____

_____

_____

_____

_____

_____

_____

_____

_____

_____

_____

_____

_____

_____

_____

_____

Draw a Croquis Figure

A croquis, pronounced *kroh-kee*, is a French word for sketch. The figure opposite is a croquis.

The pages that follow have pre-made croquis figures for you to style, but it's fun to try drawing them on your own. Spend time getting comfortable before moving on. Don't worry. Practice makes pretty. Everyone starts here!

1 Gather materials: pencil, ruler and plain (unruled) 8½ x 11 inch or A4 sheets of paper.

2 Fold paper in half lengthwise.

3 Create guidelines. Use your ruler to draw eight horizontal lines an equal distance apart (about 1 inch / 2.5 cm) along the folded line.

4 Draw a balance line. Use your ruler to trace over the center folded (vertical) line.

5 Fill in the fashion figure. Use the guidelines and balance lines to create the human shape. Start by making stick-figure-like lines or blocking it out.

6 Repeat: Try it again! Carry on until you feel comfortable, each time making smoother and smoother lines.

— TIP —

Practice drawing fashion with a real life model! Ask your friends or a family member to pose standing in different ways while you draw. Remember to create your guidelines before starting.

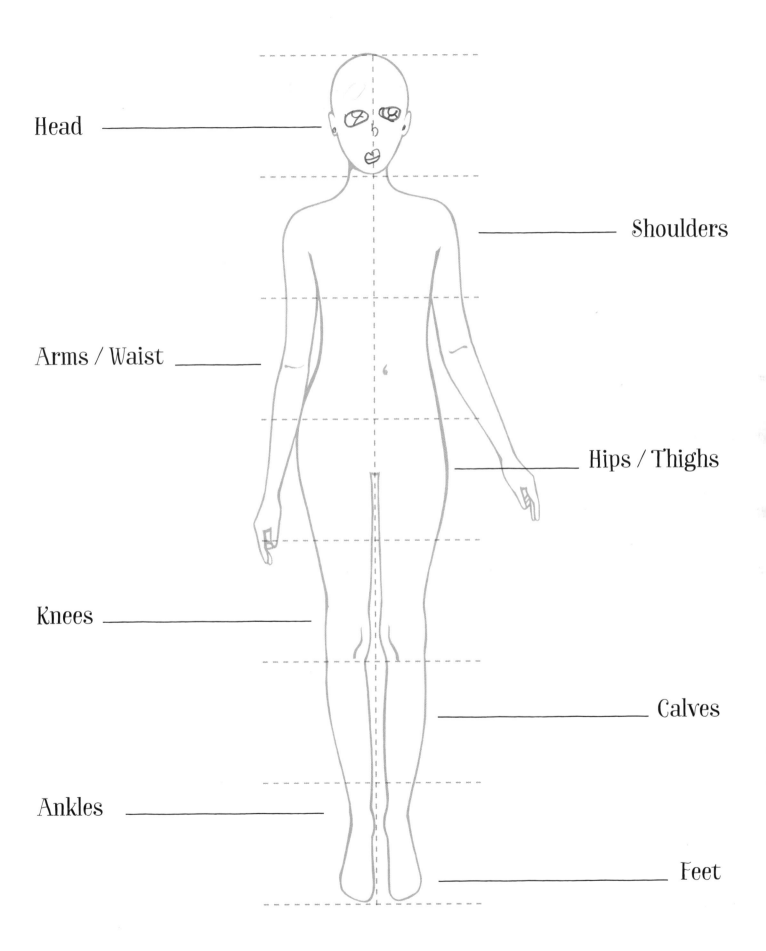

Head ——————————

Shoulders ——————

Arms / Waist ————

Hips / Thighs ——————

Knees ——————————

Calves ——————

Ankles ——————————

Feet ——————

Draw Clothes

Use these four easy steps to help you create fashionable looks on your croquis.

1 Find the shapes in the garment you want to draw

2 Draw the shapes the right size

3 Now curve the lines to the shape of the body

4 Add shading

Now try using this sundress:

Look for the shapes. The straps are rectangles and the bodice two triangles. The waistband is another rectangle and the skirt a triangle with the top cut off.

Draw the shapes again. This time curve the lines.

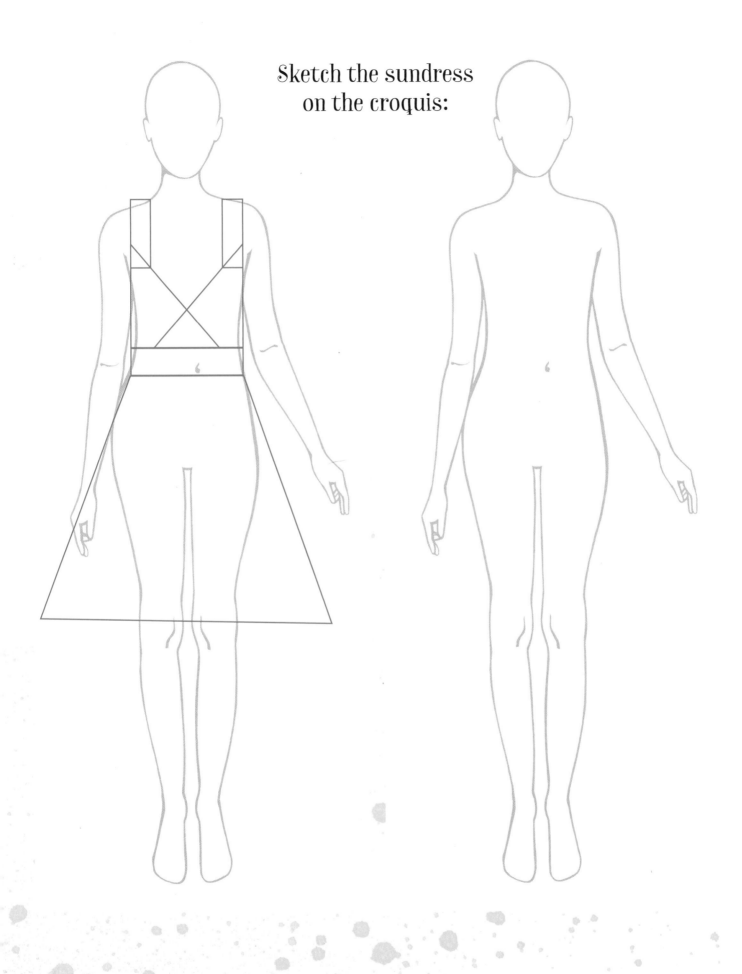

Sketch the sundress
on the croquis:

Make Faces

Rely on shapes to make a face. Here are some tips as you create.

HEAD

★ Start with an oval. Divide by a center line and then across

★ Mark the hairline about halfway between the top of the head and the eyebrows. Add some hair like a simple tendril, wisp, or twist!

EYES

★ Eyes are about one eye width apart

★ Eyes are about half as tall as they are wide

★ Eyes are in the middle of the head

★ Eyebrows are the same length as the top of the eye

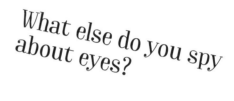

NOSE

★ Noses are about halfway between the eyes and the chin

MOUTH

★ Mouths usually stretch from the center of one eye to the other

Remember each face is different. Don't try to match these measurements exactly. They are just suggestions to help you draw it yourself!

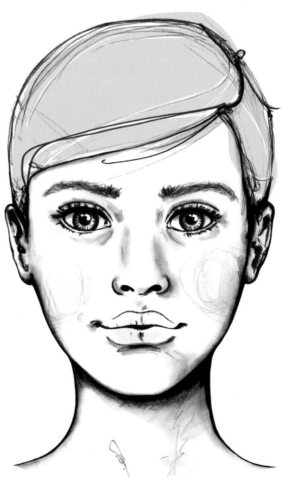

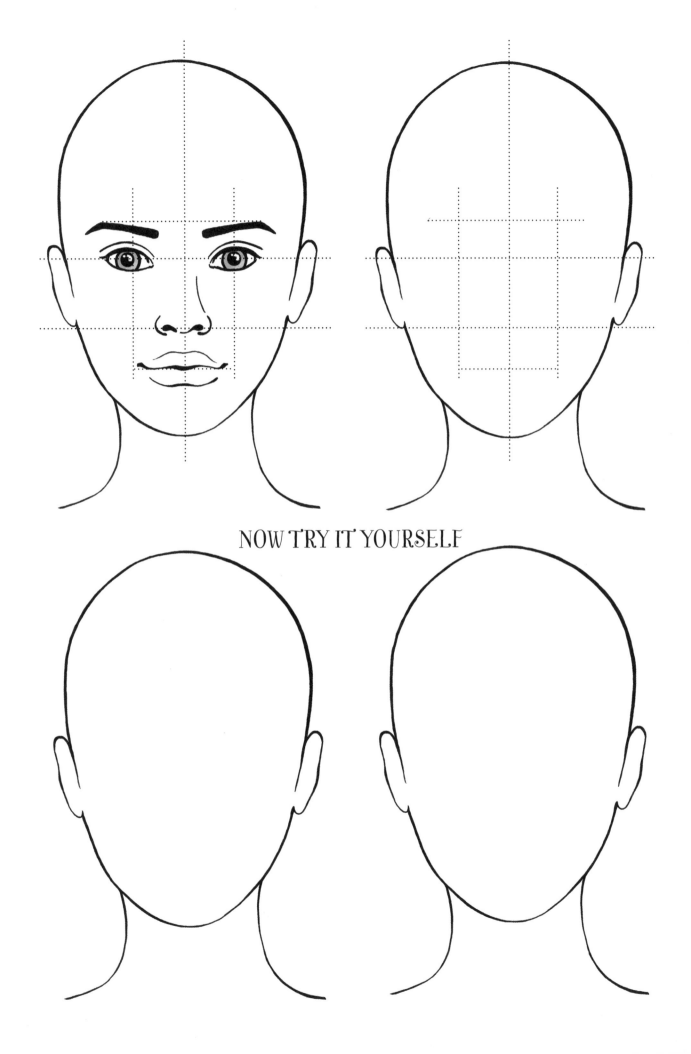

NOW TRY IT YOURSELF

Elements of Design

Meet the four elements of design. They can be tricky at first but once you get the hang you'll be able to create a style that stands out in the crowd! Here's the scoop.

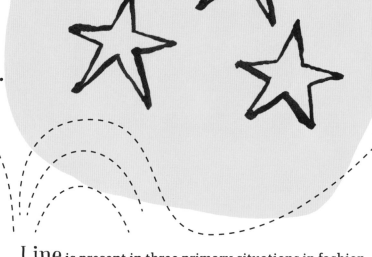

Color is the most important element of design. Think about what colors you use and know which ones look good on you.

Silhouette is the shape that a garment or accessory creates. For example, wearing a tutu gives you the silhouette of a ballerina!

Line is present in three primary situations in fashion:

1 Seam lines (the lines formed when you stitch)

2 To make up the fabric pattern or print

3 The silhouette

Texture is created by using different varieties of fabric and trims.

Understanding prints and types of materials like silk, wool, fur, and linen will help you create a different texture in your designs.

Now create an
outfit or two using
all four elements.

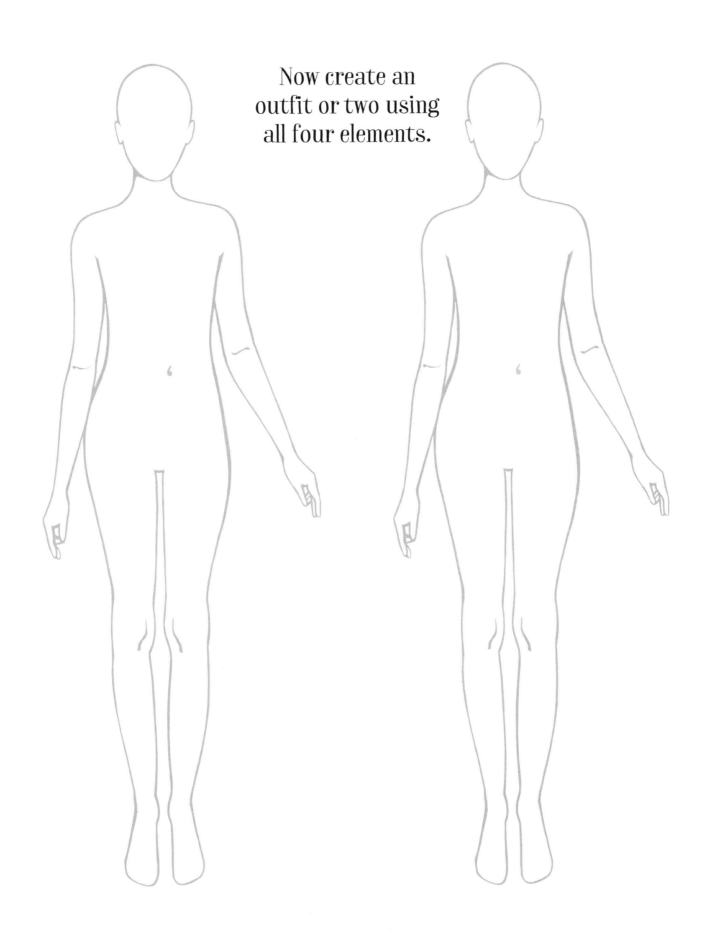

Draw the Elements

Next add your twist to create four different looks using color, silhouette, line, and texture. Note below which elements you used.

_____   _____

_____   _____

_____   _____

_____   _____

Color Hunt

Look everywhere for inspiration! Draw, paint, and paste in all the shades of each color you can find. Look at cereal packets, magazines, or your favorite nail polish colors.

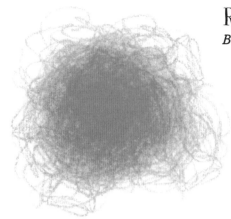

RED
Burgundy, Cherry, Crimson, Maroon, Ruby, Tomato

ORANGE
Apricot, Burnt, Carrot, Coral, Pumpkin

PINK
Fuchsia, Hot Pink, Magenta, Pastel, Salmon

YELLOW
Chartreuse, Gold, Honey, Lemon, Sunflower

GREEN
Emerald, Forest, Kelly, Lime, Olive, Pear, Sea Foam

BLUE
Baby, Denim, Light Blue, Navy, Royal, Sky

PURPLE
Eggplant (Aubergine), Lavender, Lilac, Violet

NEUTRAL
Black, Brown, Denim, Gray, Ivory, White

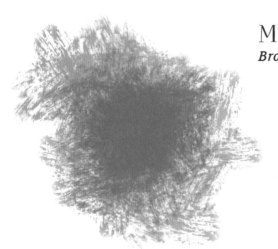

METALLIC
Bronze, Gold, Silver, Rose Gold, Glitter

Color Blocking

Color blocking means wearing two or more solid colors in one outfit to create a bold look. These color combinations are usually easy to see from a distance.

There are "sew" many cool ways to Color Block!

Imagine what colors will make a happy pair.

Think of combinations like an icy blue top with tricycle red bottoms or a pale pink dress with a pair of fiery orange tights.

Shop your own closet for solid pieces—experiment!

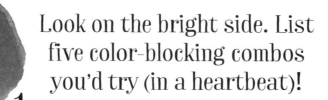

Look on the bright side. List five color-blocking combos you'd try (in a heartbeat)!

1 _____

2 _____

3 _____

4 _____

5 _____

Select eight colors to create four different color
color blocks below.

Fashion Capitals

Fashion capitals are cities that have major influences on fashion trends around the world. These cities are usually responsible for designing, producing, and selling lots of fashion. They hold special events like fashion weeks and fairs too.

- New York City, USA
- Paris, France
- London, England
- Milan, Italy
- Barcelona, Spain
- Beijing, China
- Berlin, Germany
- Lagos, Nigeria
- Tokyo, Japan

Fashion Seasons

Fashion has two seasons, Spring/Summer (S/S) and Fall (Autumn)/Winter (F/W). The collections are presented on the catwalk during the major fashion weeks six months in advance, so that buyers who work for the stores have time to get them in stock.

These cities hold major fashion shows every spring and fall.

LOCATION	SHOW MONTHS	TIME ZONE	
NEW YORK, USA	SEPTEMBER/FEBRUARY	12 NOON	
LONDON, ENGLAND	SEPTEMBER/FEBRUARY	5 PM	
MILAN, ITALY	SEPTEMBER/FEBRUARY	6 PM	
PARIS, FRANCE	SEPTEMBER (OCTOBER)/ FEBRUARY (MARCH)	6 PM	

Other cities to see amazing fashion

- ★ Antwerp, Belgium
- ★ Florence, Italy
- ★ Helsinki, Finland
- ★ Johannesburg, South Africa
- ★ Madrid, Spain
- ★ Miami, Florida, USA
- ★ Montreal, Quebec, Canada
- ★ Seoul, South Korea
- ★ Sydney, Australia
- ★ _____
- ★ _____
- ★ _____

Add your favorite fashion-forward cities to the list.

Place a ✔ next to the cities that you've visited and a ❤ beside those you'd love to explore.

My Seasonal Fashion

Write, draw, paint, or paste fashion inspiration for each of the four seasons.

SPRING
What makes your spring a breeze?

SUMMER
What do you wear on the sun-days of summer?

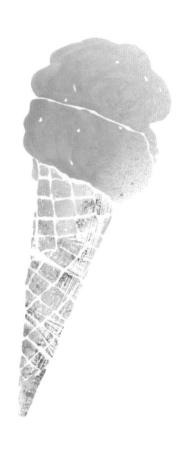

FALL / AUTUMN
How do you turn over a new leaf?

WINTER
How do you gear up for winter?

Fashion Timeline

You don't need a time machine to draw inspiration from the past. Check out this fashion history timeline told through silhouettes, starting in the 1900s.

1900

Silhouette: Slimming, fewer undergarments, loosened corsets, high-waist gowns, well constructed (beading, tucking, insertions, appliqués).

Popular Designer: Paul Poiret (Born: Paris, France)

1910

Silhouette: Fluid and soft with less boning on dresses. Hem of skirts rose to ankle, draping on dresses.

Popular Designer: Jacques Doucet (Born: Paris, France)

1920

Silhouette: Simplicity. Loose, shorter hemlines, lightweight fabrics.

Popular Designer: Coco Chanel (Born: Saumur, France)

1930

Silhouette: Longer skirts, single scoop or V-necklines, fur on coats. Fashion inspired by Hollywood starlets.

Popular Designer: Madame Grès (Born: Paris, France)

1940

Silhouette: Shoulder gathering, V-necklines, shorter skirts, and practicality.

Popular Designer: Christian Dior (Born: Granville, France)

1950

Silhouette: Fitted and short but also loose and free with wide skirts, structural garments, cinched waists.

Popular Designer: Cristóbal Balenciaga (Born: Getaria, Spain)

1960

Silhouette: Empire-line dresses, structured, clean cut, shorter skirts, baby-doll look.

Popular Designer: Emilio Pucci (Born: Florence, Italy)

1970

Silhouette: Maxi, mini, or midi-skirts, flared trousers, exotic and tropical prints, halter necklines, punk fashion.

Popular Designer: Roy Halston Frowick (Born: Des Moines, Iowa, USA)

1980

Silhouette: "Power dressing," shoulder pads, structured, daring (underwear was outerwear), revealing necklines, romantic.

Popular Designer: Calvin Klein (Born: New York City, USA)

1990

Silhouette: Comfort, loose fitting, colorful or punk, dark colors, industrial and military styles.

Popular Designer: Jean Paul Gaultier (Born: Arcueil, France)

2000

Silhouette: Plunging necklines, long hippie-inspired skirts and dresses, corset tops, revealing.

Popular Designer: Alexander McQueen (Born: London, United Kingdom)

2010

Silhouette: Anything goes, from revealing (skinny jeans) to "boyfriend" cuts (oversized). Lots of vintage and vintage-inspired pieces.

Popular Designer: Marc Jacobs (Born: New York City, USA)

The Future

What do you think future fashions will look like? Draw and write your ideas here.

_____

_____

_____

_____

Chart Your Fashion Timeline

Use a combination of photos, words, and drawings to chart your fashion history. What were the top fashion moments in your life? Include some moments that may have been slightly embarrassing, that you learned from, too!

YEAR:
FASHION MOMENT:

YEAR:
FASHION MOMENT:

YEAR:
FASHION MOMENT:

YEAR:
FASHION MOMENT:

YEAR:
FASHION MOMENT:

YEAR:
FASHION MOMENT:

Multiple Choice

Fashion trends change really fast, but there's no need to fret or keep up with the fads. Wearing pieces over and over is a sign of style. Draw or cut and paste your fashion must-haves. What are the garments or accessories that are true to you?

Fantastic Fabric

Polka Dot

Paisley

Tie Dye

Tiny Floral

Tartan

Large Floral

Herringbone

Zebra

Hearts

Houndstooth

Toile

Sequin

Pinstripe

Gingham

Argyle

Snake

Stripe

Harlequin

Novelty

Camouflage

Have Fun with Fabric!

What patterns can you think of? Create your own printed swatches and work them into a design.

— TIP —

Novelty prints, also called conversation-starter prints, are printed with a theme or motif that could represent animals, food, and other colorful ideas.

Play with polka dots! Can you use different-size circles to create an innovative new polka-dot print?

Use concentration and size to make new prints using only straight lines. Try diagonals, pinstripes, checks, chevrons, plaids, and super checks.

Style List

Say "ciao" to your fashion style list! You are almost ready to "draw it yourself."

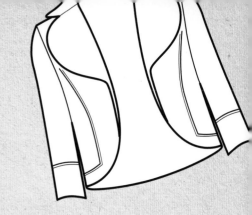

Frock Shop

Imagine your dream dress and then design it!
Sketch a draft on a piece of drawing paper.
Draw the final version on the croquis on the
next page.

Ballgown

Strapless

Pleated

A draft is a version of
something, like a drawing,
that you make before you
create the final.

Shift

Hi-Low

Shirt

Maxi

Sundress

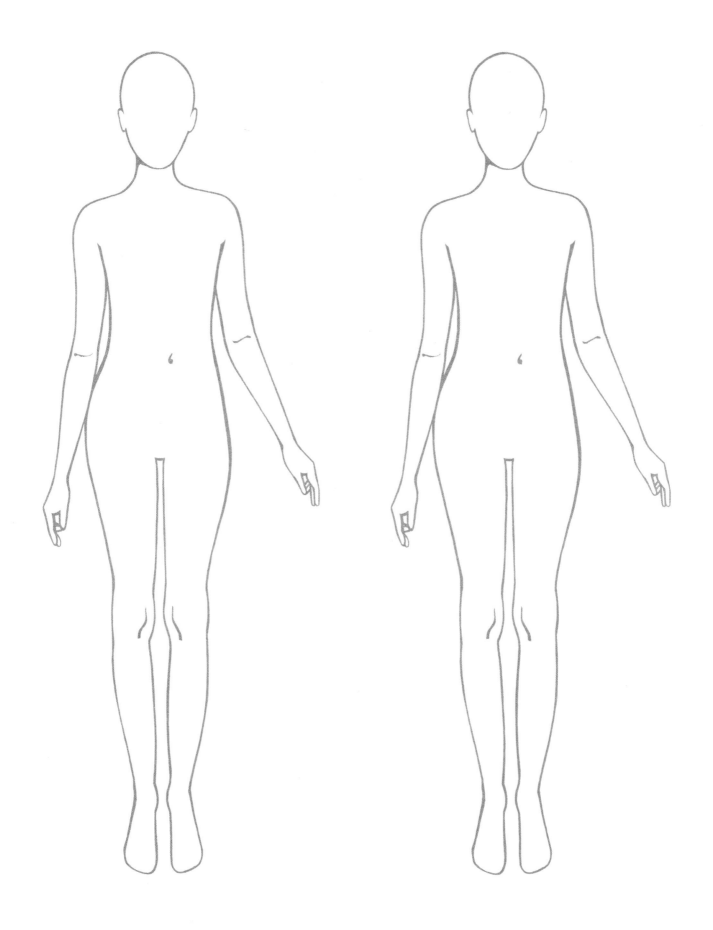

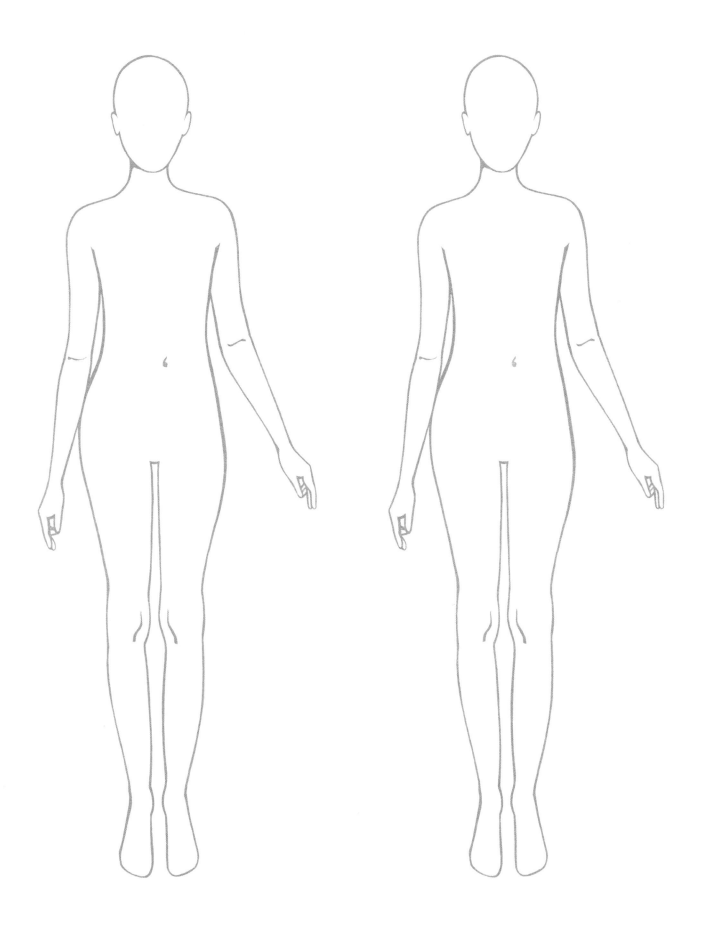

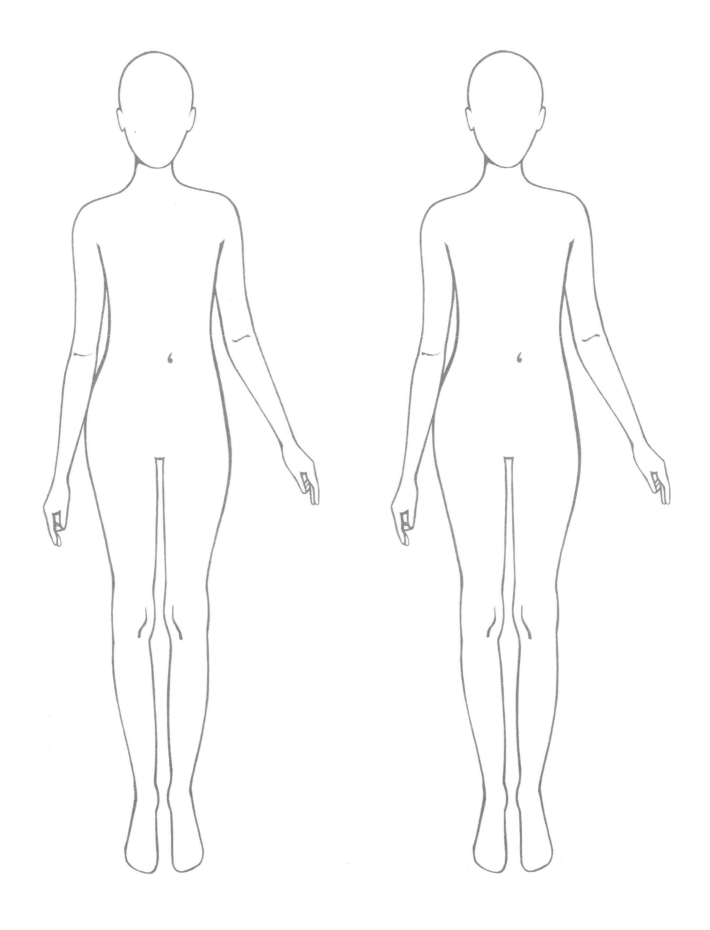

New Necklines to Try

(With tops and dresses)

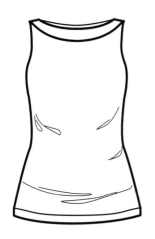

Boat Neck

Halter Neck

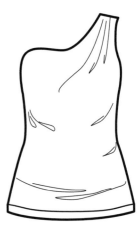

Sailor Collar

One Shoulder

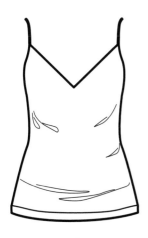

Spaghetti
Strap

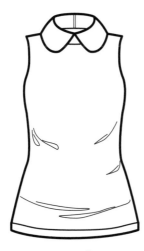

Peter Pan
Collar

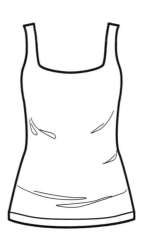

Square Neck

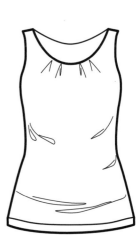

Scoop Neck

— **TIP** —

Add fashionable finishing touches
like zippers, buttons, pockets, and
appliqué. Take a look in your own
closet (wardrobe) for inspiration.

Fashion Zodiac

The world would be hard to imagine without fashion. It's just as hard to imagine the sky without stars. Let's look to the stars for some out-of-this-world inspiration!

Aries
March 21–April 19
Be a trendsetter; shine bright. Resist the urge to spend on trends because you will quickly be bored. Stand out from the crowd by learning to DIY trendy accessories and start to buy second-hand.
- Gemstone: Diamond
- Color to love: Red
- Countries to explore: England, France, Germany

Taurus
April 20–May 20
You are warm-hearted and loving. It's okay to stick with the brands and designers you adore, but go ahead and try something new. Have fun with your fashion!
- Gemstone: Emerald
- Colors to love: Pink and other pastel shades
- Countries to explore: Ireland, Cyprus

Gemini
May 21–June 20
You have a brilliant knack for communicating and versatility comes naturally to you. Share thoughts, ideas, and drawings from this book with friends for their feedback. Continue your study of fashion!
- Gemstone: Agate
- Color to love: Yellow
- Countries to explore: Wales, USA, Egypt

Cancer
June 21–July 22
You are intuitive and imaginative. You know what's in fashion before it's a trend! Fashion can affect your mood, so be smart about what you wear. Clothe yourself in colors that make you happy. Develop your appreciation of music; it goes hand-in-hand with fashion.
- Gemstone: Pearl
- Colors to love: Silver and gray
- Countries to explore: Ghana, Egypt, Scotland

Leo
July 23–August 22
You are creative, ambitious, and not afraid to take the stage (or the catwalk). You can be generous with your possessions, making you an adored BFF to many. Be as you are and have fun in the sun!
- Gemstone: Ruby
- Colors to love: Anything that looks like the sun!
- Countries to explore: Italy, Sicily, South of France

Virgo
August 23–September 22
Your attention to detail will take you far! After you finish your homework, put your energy into fashion. Use your ability to be neat to organize your wardrobe, accessories, and inspiration for your style files. Be careful not to let your perfectionism give you angst. There's no such thing as bad luck.
- Gemstone: Sardonyx
- Colors to love: Navy blue, brown, and green
- Countries to explore: Greece, the West Indies, Jordan, Brazil

Libra
September 23–October 22
You seek harmony in all aspects of life and this shows in what you wear. You are dreamy, easy to get along with, and social. Don't ever be afraid to make a choice. Have fun wearing fashionable art!
- Gemstones: Sapphire and jade
- Colors to love: Different hues of blue, pink, sea-foam green
- Countries to explore: Japan, Argentina, China, Austria

Scorpio

October 23–November 21

Scorpios are known for their passion, and when they love fashion it can be amazing! Write goals for yourself. With effort you can do anything you set your mind to. Put on your seatbelt and ride the whimsical rollercoaster of fashion.

- Gemstone: Opal
- Colors to love: Dark reds
- Countries to explore: Morocco, Norway, Korea

Sagittarius

November 22–December 21

You are always up for a challenge making you great at sewing, styling, and thrift shopping. You can be restless, so always keep a DIY project in the works. You have a keen interest in fashion. Figure out what aspect you love and go for it!

- Gemstone: Topaz
- Colors to love: Dark blue and purple
- Countries to explore: Spain, Australia, South Africa

Capricorn

December 22–January 19

You look amazing in contrasting colors and patterns. You are responsible and tend to take care of your things, giving you the ability to relate well with others, including adults. You are loyal to the brands and designers that look good on you.

- Gemstone: Turquoise
- Colors to love: Black and dark gray
- Countries to explore: India, Mexico

Aquarius

January 20–February 18

You are prone to do your own thing when it comes to fashion. You love helping friends and family with their shopping. You like to broaden your fashion horizons and explore.

- Gemstone: Aquamarine
- Color to love: Turquoise
- Countries to explore: Russia, Germany

Pisces

February 19–March 20

You are cheerful and sweet. You like to take on fun fashion projects and get others involved. Use your technical flair to come up with innovative and even scientific ways to improve fashion.

- Gemstone: Moonstone
- Color to love: Sea green
- Countries to explore: Portugal, Mediterranean islands, the Sahara Desert

Super Tops and Skirts

Skirts and tops are the issue. How will you style them?

Blouse

T-Shirt

Tank

Vest

Gypsy

Hoodie

Button Down

Sweater

Why not create an outfit using a combination of shades you created on the color blocking page?

A Line

Circle

Mini

Maxi

Straight

Tiered

Tutu

Pleated

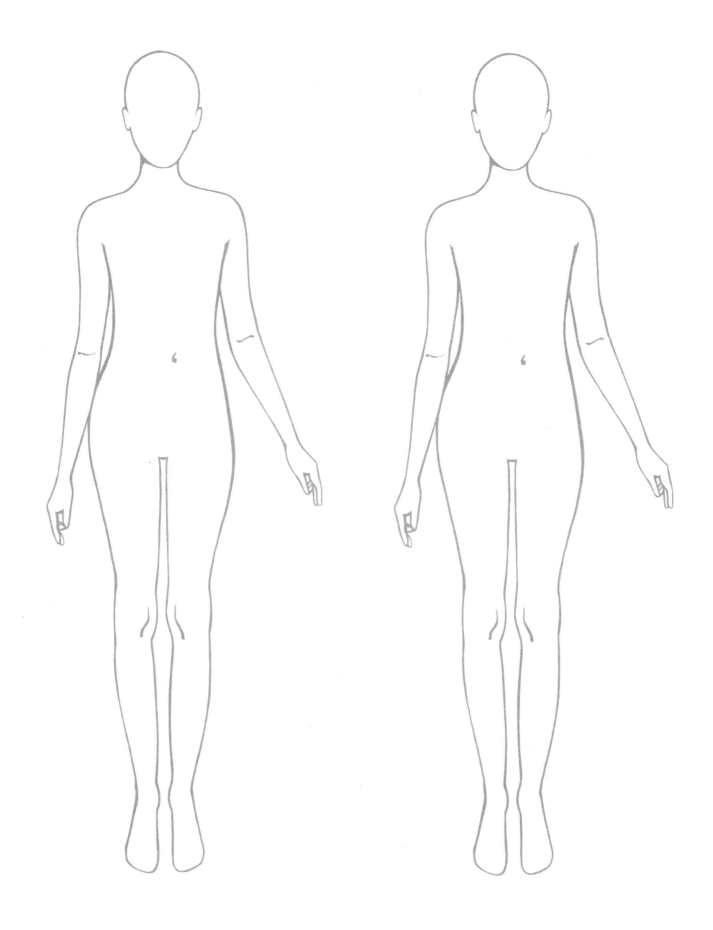

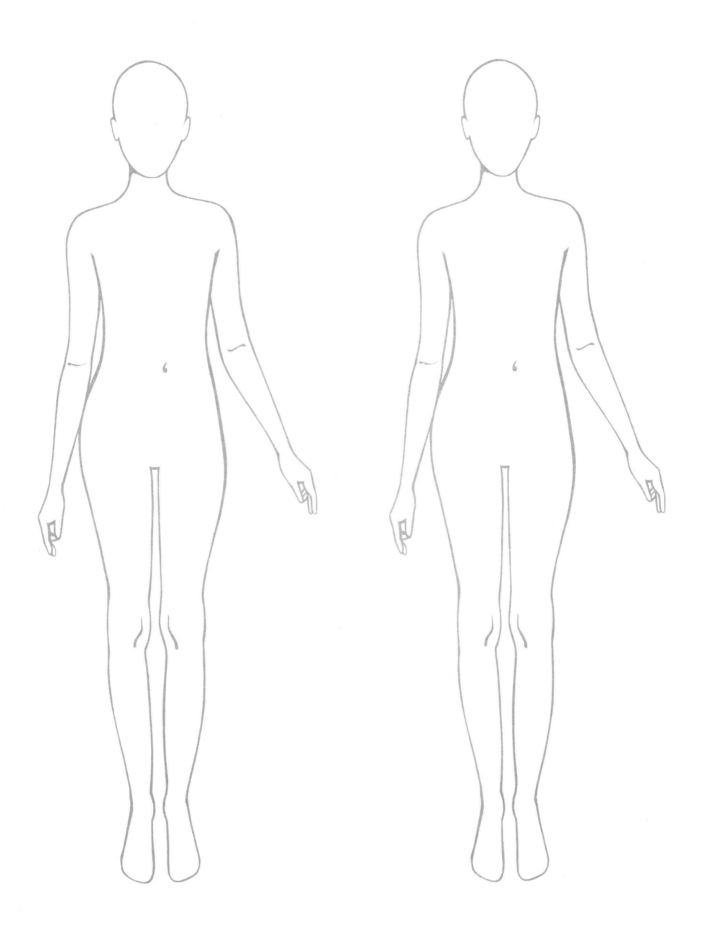

Terrific Trousers

Choose from an array of styles and tailor-make your trousers. Go ahead and throw a fit!

Cargo Pants

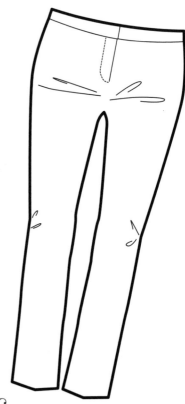

Capri Pants

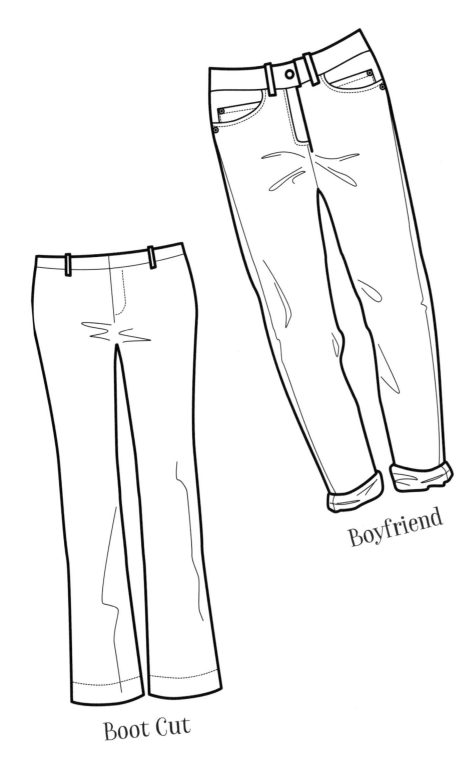

Boot Cut

Boyfriend

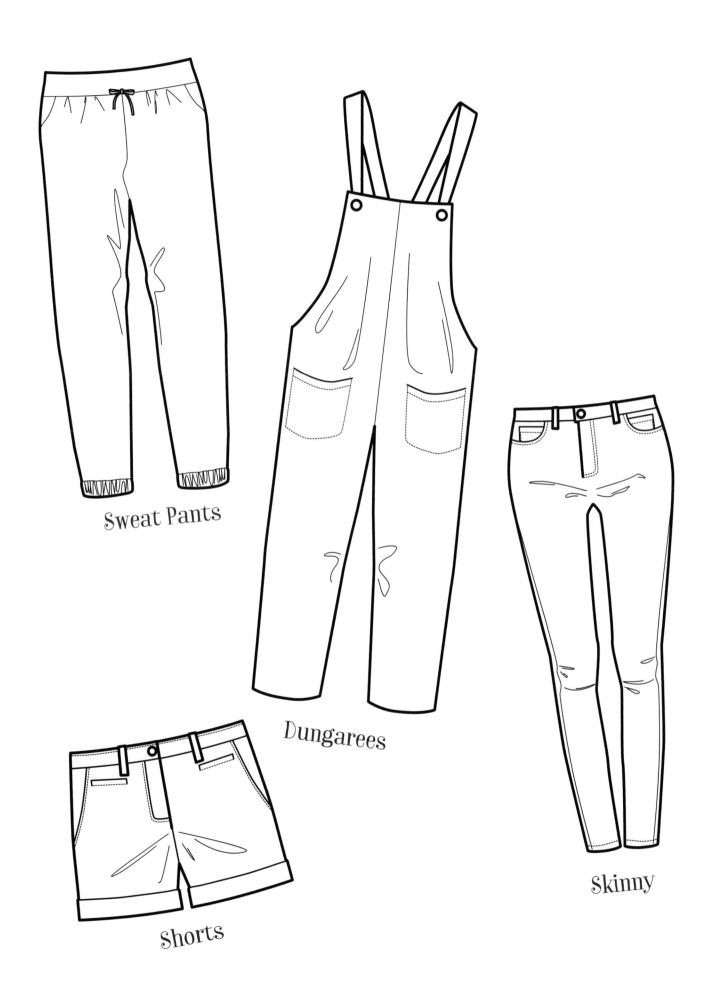

Sweat Pants

Dungarees

Shorts

Skinny

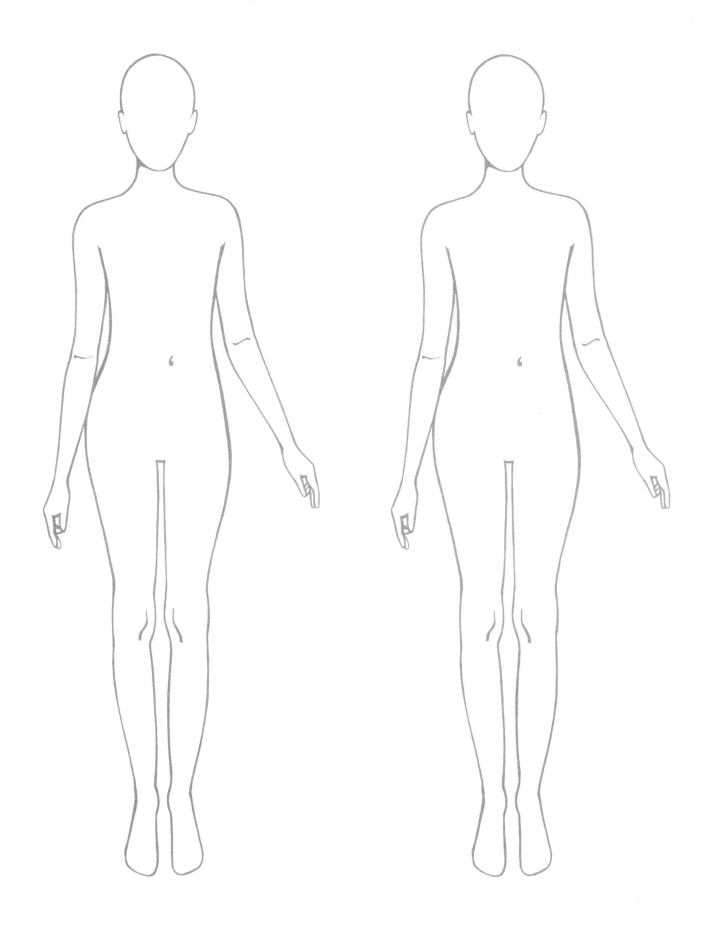

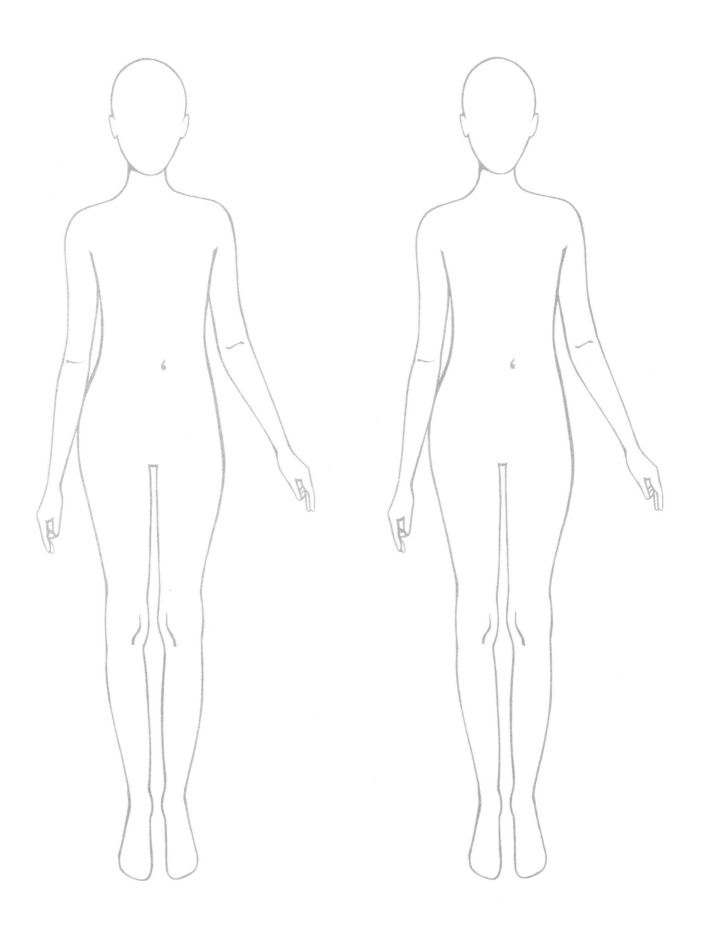

Outerwear

Create a style storm.... Use creative colors
and happy hues.

Blazer

Baby Doll
Coat

Quilted/Puffer Coat

Bolero Jacket

Denim Jacket

Cape

Parka

Peacoat

Accessories

If your shoes could talk, where would they tell you to walk?

Cowboy
Boots

Mary Janes

Peep Toes

Combat
Boots

Basketball
Boots

Slip Ons

Chunky Heels

Espadrilles

Hats, bags, and belts are the best!

Beanie

Sunhat

Cloche

Cross Body Bag

Beret

Fedora

Belt

Tote

Frame on you!

Geometric

Cateye

Aviator

Preppy/Boston

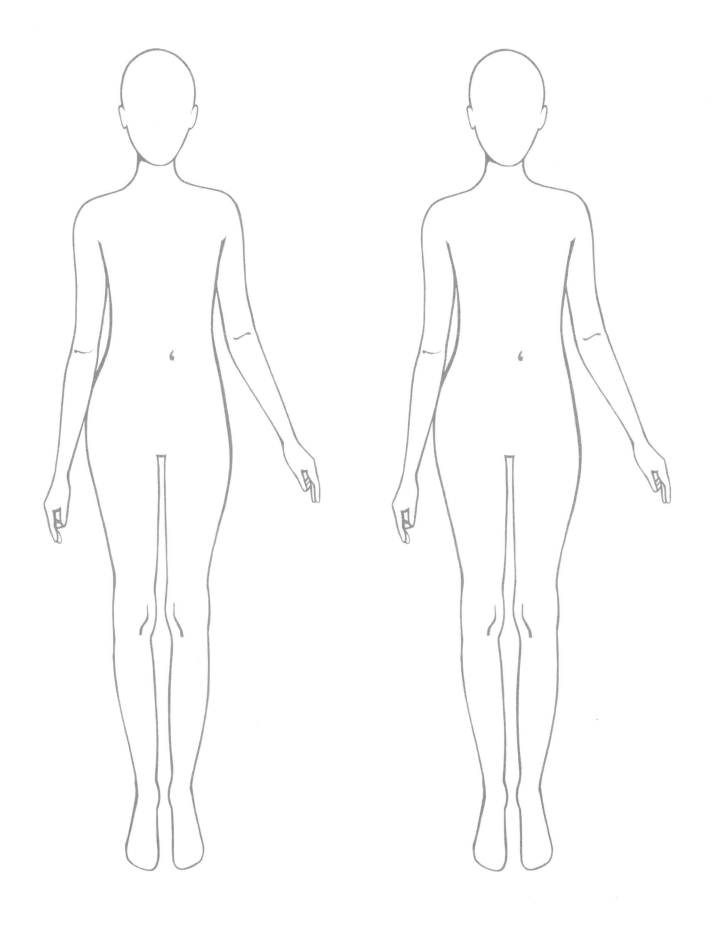

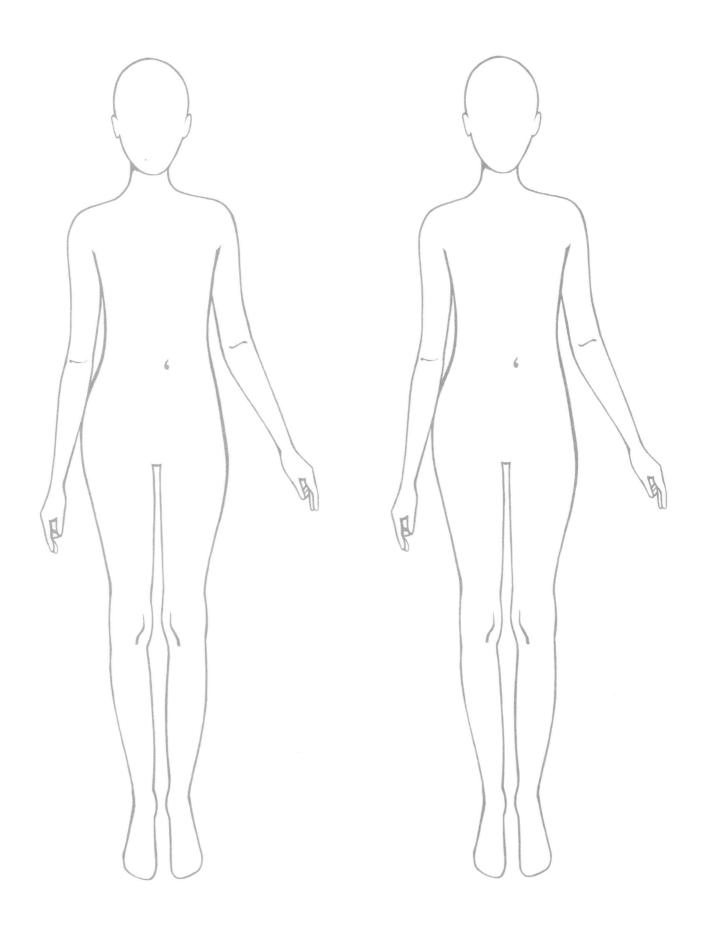

Sum Up Your Style

Don't forget the details on the back of the outfit you're drawing.

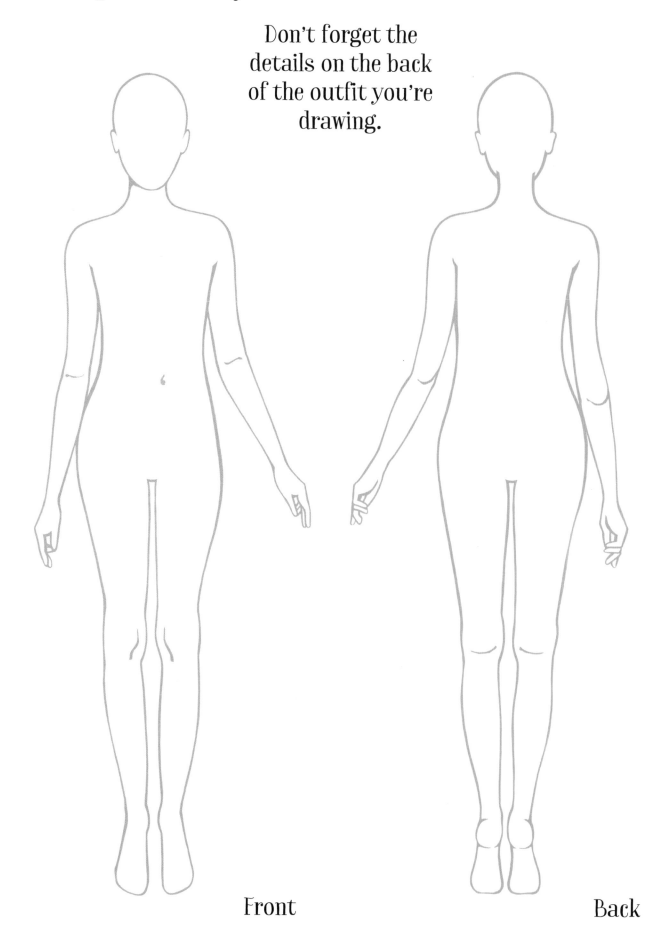

Front

Back

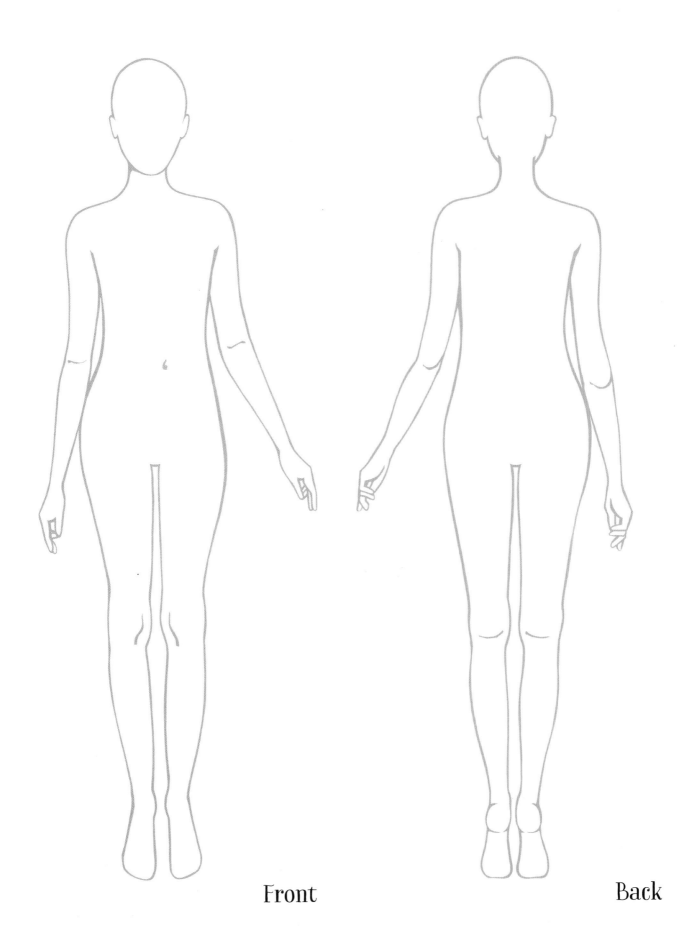

Front   Back

You've Got Mail

Write a letter to your future self.
Describe your style, or how you dress for success, and include some
of your hopes and goals for your fashion future.

Seal it with an "XO."

Lingo in Different Languages

A few words and phrases for fashionistas to understand, because you never know where your style could lead you!

French

À la mode	Fashionable
Avant-garde	Innovative
Boutique	Small shop
Cap-à-pied	From head to toe
Chic	Smart or stylish
Haute couture	High fashion
J'adore	I adore
Je ne sais quoi	A certain something
Modéliste	Fashion designer
Prêt-à-porter	Ready-to-wear
Vogue	Fashion

J'adore

Ciao

Italian

Ciao	Hello *or* goodbye
Da morire	To die for
La passerella	The runway (catwalk)
Vogliamo fare "shopping"	We want to go shopping

Spanish

Elegante	Stylish
La belleza cuesta	It hurts to be pretty
Pasado de moda	Out of fashion
Seguir la moda	To follow fashion
Vestido	Dress
Zapatillas	Shoes

Elegante

All your dreams can be real.
Practice, practice, practice–until they come
true. It's miraculous and up to you!

Stop Press

Your own collection is featured in your favorite magazine. What's the headline? Add pictures, too. Who was sitting in the front row of your fashion show? Why not try mixing in fashion words in different languages?

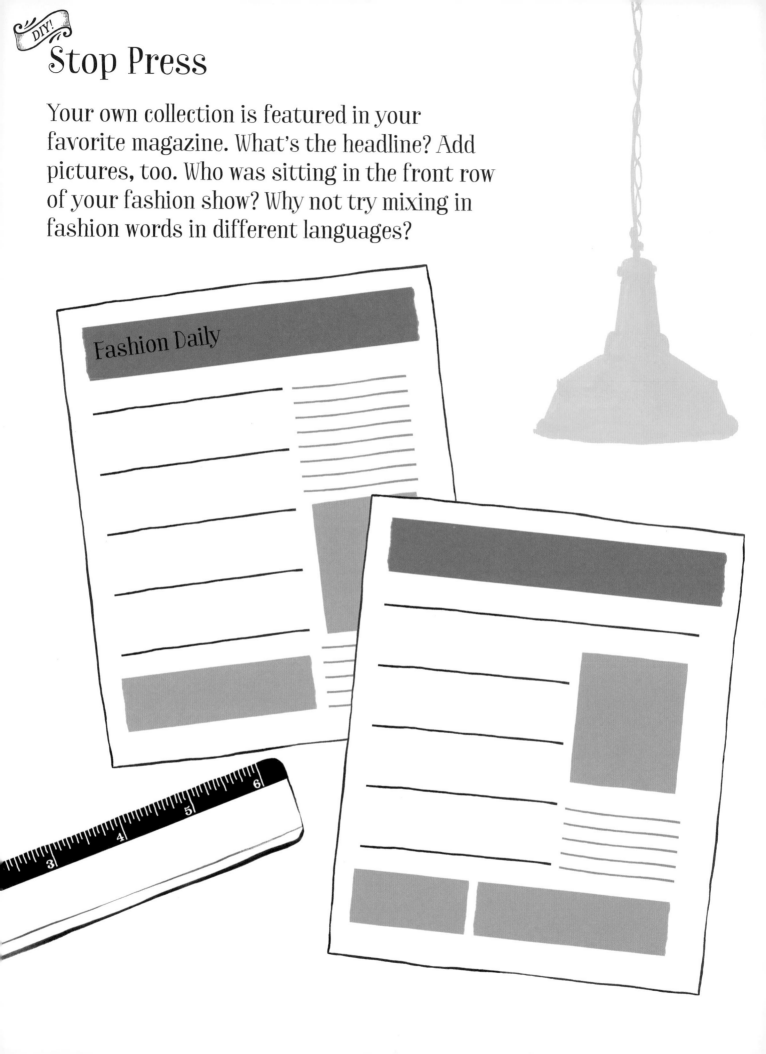

Fashion Daily

Designer Names to Know

Alexander McQueen (1969–2010) was famous for macabre designs including skull prints. He also invented low-rise jeans.

Betsey Johnson (1942–) is known for her exuberant, whimsical, and sometimes over the top designs for women.

Calvin Klein (1942–) designs clothes for both men and women, but is most famous for his jeans.

Christian Dior (1905–1957) was most known for his first collection, in 1947, called "The New Look" which was a major shift in post-World War II fashion. This new look was embraced by women all over the world.

Christian Siriano (1985–) is known for his show-stopping evening gowns and cocktail dresses. He is the youngest designer to win the TV show Project Runway.

Coco Chanel (1883–1971) was famous for many fab things. Her designs went beyond garments and included jewelry, handbags, and fragrances, including her signature scent Chanel No. 5.

Cristóbal Balenciaga (1895–1972) was called the "Picasso of Fashion" for his artistic take on shape (silhouette) and form. Black, red, and pink were his favorite colors.

Diane von Furstenberg (1946–) is famous for the iconic, easy-to-wear, wrap dress.

Donna Karan (1948–) is best known for creating comfortable, simple, elegant clothing for women that makes it easy for them to get dressed.

Emilio Pucci (1914–1992) was renowned for his delightful kaleidoscope-like prints.

Jacques Doucet (1853–1929) was born in Paris into a fashion-industry family. He was known for his elegant dresses, and also had an impressive collection of fine art.

LIVE YOUR PASSION BE A SUCCESS

Jean Paul Gaultier (1952–) is especially known for the creation of modernized corsets (and bras) in the early 1990s.

Karl Lagerfeld (1933–) is the head designer and creative director for the Chanel brand. He has a cat named Choupette.

Madame Grès (1903–1993) was known for her ability to sculpt fabric using tiny pleats, making timeless pieces.

Marc Jacobs (1963–) is best known for his fashion design with Louis Vuitton and his own label Marc by Marc Jacobs. He has a tattoo of SpongeBob SquarePants on his right arm.

Mary Quant (1934–) is credited with many fashion innovations in the 1960s, including the miniskirt and waterproof mascara.

Michael Kors (1959–) is best known for his opinionated comments on the reality TV show Project Runway.

Ozwald Boateng (1967–) made his mark with impeccable tailoring on menswear.

Paul Poiret (1879–1944) was a popular French designer during the first two decades of the twentieth century. In America he was known as "The King of Fashion." In Paris, he was simply "Le Magnifique."

Roy Halston Frowick (1932–1990), known as "Halston," was popular in the 1970s. He created simple dresses that became favorites in American discos.

Stella McCartney (1971–) is one of the most outspoken fashion designers in the world. She is an animal rights activist who never uses leather, animal skins, or fur in any of her creations.

Tom Ford (1961–) is famous for his design work with the Gucci brand, the creation of the Tom Ford label, and directing an Oscar-nominated film.

Tracy Reese (1964–) is best known for her retro-inspired dresses and her playful twist on modern womenswear.

Vera Wang (1949–) blends traditional and modern details to create stunning bridal wear.

Vivienne Westwood (1941–) became famous in the 1970s when her early fashion designs helped shape the look of the punk movement.

Zac Posen (1980–) is best known for being called fashion's "next big thing" at just 21 years old.

Room to Grow

Growing does not have to be a pain. Learn the whos, whats, and *wears* of clothing sizing and care with this handy size converter.

Highlight your size!

Clothing by age

AGE	8	10	12	14	16
HEIGHT (IN.)	51–53	54–57	58–60	61–63	64–66
HEIGHT (CM.)	130–135	137–145	147–152	155–160	161–167

Clothing by size

USA	0	2	4	6	8
EUROPE	32	34	36	38	40
UK	4	6	8	10	12

USA	10	12	14	16
EUROPE	42	44	46	48
UK	14	16	18	20

Shoe sizes

USA	4½	5	5½	6	6½	7	7½	8
EUROPE	34	35	35½	36	37	37½	38	38½
UK	2	2½	3	3½	4	4½	5	5½

USA	8½	9	9½	10	10½	11
EUROPE	39	40	41	42	43	44
UK	6	6½	7	7½	8	9

Four Tips to Help Care for your Clothes

1 Close zippers and other fasteners before putting your dirty clothes in the laundry basket. This will prevent your other clothes from getting damaged.

2 Separate colors from the whites.

3 Empty your pockets of paper and other random things (like lip gloss or crayons) that can make your laundry a big mess.

4 Read the care label, inside your garments, to save your clothes from an accidental disaster. See below for what the symbols stand for.

Be good to your clothes and your clothes will be good to you!

MACHINE WASH	⊔	**IRON ANY TEMP**	⌐
HAND WASH	⊔	**NO IRON**	⊠
TUMBLE DRY ANY HEAT	⊡	**DRY CLEAN**	◯
DO NOT TUMBLE DRY	⊠	**DO NOT DRY CLEAN**	⊗
ANY BLEACH	△	**DO NOT WRING**	⋈
NO BLEACH	⊿	**LAY FLAT TO DRY**	⊟

— TIP —

Keep six tops and six bottoms that you like to wear clean. That way you'll only have to do the laundry once a week. Neat!

You are a Fashion Star!

Play a starring role—write what you'll do.
Remember, the future of fashion belongs
to you!

Copy or cut out the stars and embellish them
to make four *Fab Fashion* lucky charms.

With hard work your fashion wishes can come true. Why not:

learn to sew

ATTEND A FASHION SHOW

 Learn how clothes are produced

SUBSCRIBE TO A MAGAZINE

COMPLIMENT, COMPLIMENT, COMPLIMENT!

WINDOW SHOP

LOOK TO THE PAST FOR

INSPIRATION

Visit Museums

FOLLOW DESIGNERS ON SOCIAL MEDIA

SKETCH, SKETCH, SKETCH!

 BE YOU!

write fashion pieces with pizzazz

BE A FASHION DO-GOODER: SWAP CLOTHING / DONATE / UPCYCLE

JOIN
(OR START)

A FASHION CLUB

Make new friends
(or find your
style tribe)

STICK WITH IT

MAKE FASHIONABLE
ART FOR OTHERS

DO YOUR
HOMEWORK.
STUDY FASHION!

**CREATE A
FASHION ATLAS**

**INVEST
IN A
DRESS
FORM**

FIND OUT
WHERE YOUR
CLOTHES
COME FROM

Glossary

Abstract:
emphasizing lines, colors, or geometrical forms that relate to each other to create a form

Accessory:
item such as a hair clip, piece of jewelry, purse, or scarf that can be worn or carried to complete an outfit

Appliqué:
a small piece of fabric attached by hand or machine to a larger piece of fabric, to create a design

Bridal wear:
clothing for weddings

Buyer:
the job title for a person who buys clothes for stores

Career:
a job or profession

Chic:
stylish

Clothing care:
ways to be nice to your clothes

Clothing label:
a small tag inside of a garment that has the brand name or care instructions printed on it

Color:
an item's tonal quality, for example *My nails are the perfect shade of pink*

Color blocking:
a trend that involves wearing two or more solid colors in one outfit

Color scheme:
a combination of colors that work well together

Croquis:
a drawing that is quick and sketchy

DIY:
stands for "Do It Yourself" or, in this book, "Draw It Yourself"

Draft:
a version of something, like a drawing, that you make before you make the final version

Embellish:
to decorate

Fabric:
a woven or knit material made from fibers

Fashion:
is expression and beauty through clothes

Fashion capital:
a city that has a major influence on international fashion trends

Fashion designer:
a person who plans how garments look and will be made

Fashion stylist:
someone who picks out clothing for published features

Garments:
clothing

Headline:
the title written over a story in a magazine or newspaper

Inspiration:
the urge to do something creative

Line:
contours in garments made by seams, fabric prints, or silhouettes

Menswear:
clothing for men

Mood board:
an arrangement of images, materials, and pieces of text to inspire

Notable:
worth noticing

Notions (Haberdashery):
objects attached to a garment for decorative purposes or to serve a function, such as zippers, buttons, and snaps (press studs)

Print:
a textile or garment with a colored design or pattern

Runway (Catwalk):
a platform that models walk on during a fashion show

Seam:
the line that is formed, with thread, when you make a stitch

Silhouette:
the shape or outline of someone or something

Style:
how you piece together your look with fashion

Style file:
a tool to organize fashion inspiration and drawings so they can be found and used easily and quickly

Stylist:
a person whose job is to make clothing look attractive

Swatch:
a small piece of fabric

Texture:
created by using different varieties of fabric and trims

Timeline:
a graphic or drawing that shows the order of events

Trends:
what is in fashion now, and what is next

Womenswear:
clothing for women

Vintage:
styles or fashion from past decades

About the Author

Lesley Ware is an educator, style blogger, and designer living in Brooklyn, New York. In 2008, she started a blog, thecreativecookie.com, which quickly became a destination for a behind-the-scenes look at fashion in New York City. Lesley runs popular sewing and crafting workshops for girls. Her first book, *Sew Fab: Sewing and Style for Young Fashionistas*, is also published by Laurence King Publishing.

Published in 2016 by Laurence King Publishing Ltd
361–373 City Road
London EC1V 1LR
United Kingdom
Tel: +44 20 7841 6900
Fax: +44 20 7841 6910
e-mail: enquiries@laurenceking.com
www.laurenceking.com

Text © 2016 Lesley Ware

This work was produced by Laurence King Publishing Ltd, London. Lesley Ware has asserted her right under the Copyright, Designs, and Patents Act 1988, to be identified as the Author of this Work.

A catalogue record for this book is available from the British Library.
ISBN: 978-1-78067-695-1

Book design by Eleanor Ridsdale

Picture credits:
Line drawings on pages 48–51, 55, 58–59, 62–63, 66–67, and page 69 (hats, bags, and belts) by Carolyn Hewitson

Silhouettes on pages 36–38 by Eleanor Ridsdale

All other illustrations by Sabine Pieper

Photographs on pages 6, 7, 44, 45, silhouettes on page 39, and symbols page 85 by Shutterstock

Printed in China